Degenerate Art: The Exhibition Guide in German and English

By Fritz Kaiser
Berlin, 1937

Degenerate Art: The Exhibition Guide in German and English
By Fritz Kaiser
Originally published 1937

This edition 2012 by
Ostara Publications
P.O. Box 671
Burlington
IA 52601-0671
USA

www.ostarapublications.com

ISBN 978-1-4716-9274-1

Contents

Introduction..1

The Original German Guide Booklet...................................5

The Original German Guide Booklet with English
Translation...39

Introduction

In 1937, Germany's Nazi government staged an exhibition in Munich entitled "Entartete Kunst"—the official designation given to all "modern art" which was not strictly classicist or realist in nature.

The exhibition was not merely designed to illustrate what the Nazis deemed "bad art," but had a political purpose.

"Modern art" was deemed to be part of the overall assault on "German art" and culture by a Bolshevist—and largely Jewish—movement of "artists" who were working in tandem with the Communist movement to destroy German, and Western, civilization. Included in this "degenerate art" were all works classed as cubism, Dada, surrealism, symbolism, post-Impressionism and Fauvism.

In June 1937, Nazi Minister of Propaganda Joseph Goebbels put Adolf Ziegler, the head of the Reichskammer der Bildenden Künste (Reich Chamber of Visual Art), in charge of a commission tasked with confiscating all art deemed degenerate in preparation for the exhibition.

Ultimately, over 16,000 works were seized. Among the more famous "artists" classed as degenerate were Marc Chagall, Henri Matisse, Pablo Picasso and Vincent van Gogh.

Of this number, some 650 works, consisting of paintings, sculptures, prints, and books, formed part of the final exhibition which was launched in Munich on July 19, 1937.

The layout of the exhibition was deliberately designed to be as chaotic as the works themselves. Venues were chosen which accentuated the non-classicist nature of the works, all with the intention of underlining the anti-German (and hence ordered) nature of the cultural assault on western values.

The first three rooms were grouped thematically. The first room contained works considered demeaning of religion; the second featured works by Jewish artists in particular; the third contained works deemed insulting to the women, soldiers and farmers of Germany. The rest of the exhibit had no particular theme.

In each room, slogans were painted on the walls to provide a guide to the visitor:

"Insolent mockery of the Divine under Centrist rule."
"Revelation of the Jewish racial soul."
"An insult to German womanhood."
"The ideal—cretin and whore."
"Deliberate sabotage of national defense."
"German farmers—a Yiddish view."
"The Jewish longing for the wilderness reveals itself—in Germany."
"The Negro becomes the racial ideal of a degenerate art."
"Madness becomes method."
"Nature as seen by sick minds."
"Even museum bigwigs called this the 'art of the German people.'"

Labels which accompanied the works indicated how much money had been spent by museums their acquisition, so that visitors could be astonished at the price paid for some of the cruder pieces.

This was particularly relevant for items purchased during the Weimar Republic years, still fresh in the minds of all Germans. While the average German had struggled to put food in their mouths during the Great Depression, the "artistic elite" spent millions buying the works now on display and mocked for their amateurishness and crudity.

When the exhibition finally closed, this guide book, written by Fritz Kaiser, an official in the Reich Propaganda Ministry, was issued as a souvenir.

On the day before the start of the "Degenerate Art" exhibition in Munich, Adolf Hitler officially opened the "Great German Art Exhibition" at the newly-built (and still standing) House of German Art in the same city. Kaiser took portions of Hitler's opening speech to the House of German Art, and other portions of his speech to the Reich Party Congress of 1933, and wove them into the souvenir booklet—because they summed up the Nazi state's attitude on the subject so well.

Once the exhibition finally closed, many of the works were put into storage in a warehouse in Kreuzberg, Berlin. The warehouse was destroyed during the war, and the only original surviving pieces from the original confiscation efforts were those which were taken by private collectors before the destruction of the warehouse, or which were sold on auction in Switzerland and France.

Some of the works were found buried underground in Berlin at the end of the war, and they were seized and are still on display at the Hermitage Museum in St Petersburg, Russia.

In 2010, a further private collection of sculptures from the original exhibition were discovered in an underground cellar in central Berlin. These works are now on display at the Neues Museum in that city.

The Degenerate art exhibition was therefore, more than just a display of "bad art." It formed part of the National Socialist worldview and propaganda effort which sought to link modern art with degeneracy and an assault on classical values.

Minister of Propaganda Joseph Goebbels visits the exhibition.

Entartete Kunst

Original German Version

Führer

durch die Ausstellung

Entartete Kunst

Die Ausstellung wurde zusammengestellt von der Reichspropagandaleitung, Amtsleitung Kultur. Sie wird in den größeren Städten aller Gaue gezeigt werden. Verantwortlich für den Inhalt: Fritz Kaiser, München. Verlag: Verlag für Kultur- und Wirtschaftswerbung, Berlin W 35, Potsdamer Straße 59

Was will die Ausstellung „Entartete Kunst"?

Sie will am Beginn eines neuen Zeitalters für das Deutsche Volk anhand von Originaldokumenten allgemeinen Einblick geben in das grauenhafte Schlußkapitel des Kulturzerfalles der letzten Jahrzehnte vor der großen Wende.

Sie will, indem sie das Volk mit seinem gesunden Urteil aufruft, dem Geschwätz und Phrasendrusch jener Literaten- und Zunft-Cliquen ein Ende bereiten, die manchmal auch heute noch gerne bestreiten möchten, daß wir eine Kunstentartung gehabt haben.

Sie will klar machen, daß diese Entartung der Kunst mehr war als etwa nur das flüchtige Vorüberrauschen von ein paar Narrheiten, Torheiten und allzu kühnen Experimenten, die sich auch ohne die nationalsozialistische Revolution totgelaufen hätten.

Sie will zeigen, daß es sich hier auch nicht um einen „notwendigen Gärungsprozeß" handelte, sondern um einen planmäßigen Anschlag auf das Wesen und den Fortbestand der Kunst überhaupt.

Sie will die gemeinsame Wurzel der politischen Anarchie und der kulturellen Anarchie aufzeigen, die Kunstentartung als Kunstbolschewismus im ganzen Sinn des Wortes entlarven.

Sie will die weltanschaulichen, politischen, rassischen und moralischen Ziele und Absichten klarlegen, welche von den treibenden Kräften der Zersetzung verfolgt wurden.

Sie will auch zeigen, in welchem Ausmaß diese Entartungserscheinungen von den bewußt treibenden Kräften übergriffen auf mehr oder weniger unbefangene Nachbeter, die trotz einer früher schon und manchmal später wieder bewiesenen formalen Begabung gewissen-, charakter- oder instinktlos genug waren, den allgemeinen Juden- und Bolschewistenrummel mitzumachen.

Sie will gerade damit aber auch zeigen, wie gefährlich eine von ein paar jüdischen und politisch eindeutig bolschewistischen Wort-

Degenerate Art

"Kunstkommunist werden heißt zwei Phasen durchlaufen:
1. Platz in der kommunistischen Partei nehmen und die Pflichten der Solidarität im Kampf übernehmen;
2. Die revolutionäre Umstellung der Produktion vornehmen."

Der Jude Wieland Herzfelde in „Der Gegner" 1920/21.

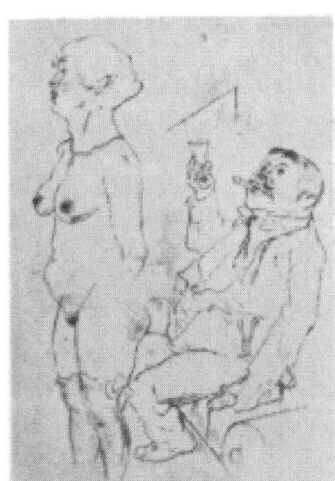

führern gelenkte Entwicklung war, wenn sie auch solche Menschen k u l t u r p o l i t i s ch in den Dienst der bolschewistischen Anarchie= pläne stellen konnte, die ein p a r t e i p o l i t i s ch e s Bekenntnis zum Bolschewismus vielleicht weit von sich gewiesen hätten.

S i e w i l l damit aber erst recht beweisen, daß heute k e i n e r der an dieser Kunstentartung damals irgendwie beteiligten Männer kommen und nur von „harmlosen Jugendeseleien" sprechen darf.

Aus alledem ergibt sich schließlich auch, was die Ausstellung „Entartete Kunst" n i ch t will:

S i e w i l l n i ch t die Behauptung aufstellen, daß a l l e Namen, die unter den ausgestellten Machwerken als Signum prangen, auch in den Mitgliederlisten der k o m m u n i s t i s ch e n P a r t e i verzeichnet waren. Diese n i ch t aufgestellte Behauptung braucht also auch n i ch t w i d e r l e g t zu werden.

S i e w i l l n i ch t bestreiten, daß der eine oder andere der hier Vertretenen manchmal — früher oder später — „auch anders gekonnt" hat. Ebensowenig aber durfte diese Ausstellung die Tat= sache verschweigen, daß solche Männer in den Jahren des bolsche= wistisch=jüdischen Generalangriffes auf die deutsche Kunst in der Front der Zersetzung standen.

S i e w i l l n i ch t verhindern, daß diejenigen Deutsch= blütigen unter den Ausgestellten, welche ihren jüdischen Freunden von ehedem nicht in das Ausland gefolgt sind, nun e h r l i ch r i n g e n und k ä m p f e n um eine Grundlage für ein neues, gesundes Schaffen. Sie w i l l und m u ß aber verhindern, daß solche Männer von den Zirkeln und Cliquen einer so düsteren Ver= gangenheit dem neuen Staat und seinem zukunftsstarken Volk gar heute schon wieder als „berufene Bannerträger einer Kunst des Dritten Reiches" aufgeschwatzt werden.

„Wir ziehen es vor, unsauber zu existieren, als sauber unterzugehen. Unfähig aber anständig zu sein, überlassen wir verbohrten Individualisten und alten Jungfern. Keine Angst um den guten Ruf!"

„Der Gegner" 1920/21.

„Das realisch Gebundene wird zerteilt und aufgebrochen zu einem Gefäß für seine aufgestaute, sinnlich brennende Leidenschaft, die — nun entzündet — keine seelische Tiefe mehr kennt und nach außen schlägt, verzehrend, expansiv, sich mit allen Teilen begattend. Es gibt für ihn keine Widerstände mehr und vorgesetzte Grenzen..."

Zeitgenössisches Literatengeschwätz über solche, damals „moderne" Bordellkunst.

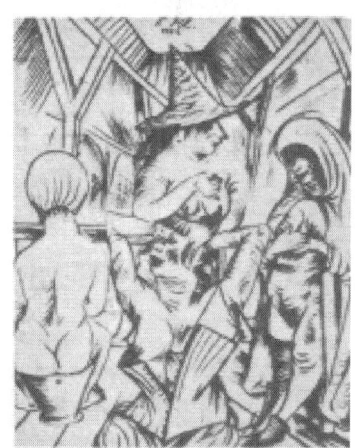

Zur Gliederung der Ausstellung

Da die Fülle der verschiedenen Entartungserscheinungen, wie sie die Ausstellung zeigen will, auf jeden Besucher ohnehin einen fast niederschmetternden Eindruck macht, wurde durch eine übersichtliche Gliederung dafür gesorgt, daß in den einzelnen Räumen jeweils der Tendenz und der Form nach zusammengehörige Werke in Gruppen übersichtlich vereinigt sind. Nachstehend wird die Führungslinie kurz dargestellt.

Gruppe 1.

Hier ist eine allgemeine Übersicht über die B a r b a r e i d e r D a r s t e l l u n g vom handwerklichen Standpunkt her zu gewinnen. Man sieht in dieser Gruppe die fortschreitende Z e r s e t z u n g d e s F o r m = u n d F a r b e m p f i n d e n s, die b e w u ß t e V e r a c h t u n g a l l e r h a n d w e r k l i c h e n G r u n d l a g e n der bildenden Kunst, die g r e l l e F a r b k l e k s e r e i neben der b e w u ß t e n V e r z e r r u n g der Zeich-

---

Wer nur das Neue sucht um des Neuen willen, verirrt sich nur zu leicht in das Gebiet der Narreteien, da das Dümmste, in Stein und Material ausgeführt, natürlich um so leichter das wirklich Neuartigste zu sein vermag, als ja in früheren Zeitaltern nicht jedem Narren genehmigt wurde, die Umwelt durch die Ausgeburten seines kranken Hirns zu beleidigen.

Der Führer
Reichsparteitag 1933.

Ein sehr aufschlußreicher

rassischer Querschnitt

Man beachte besonders auch die unten stehenden drei Malerbildnisse. Es sind von links nach rechts: Der Maler Morgner, gesehen von sich selbst. Der Maler Radziwill, gesehen von Otto Dix. Der Maler Schlemmer, gesehen von E. L. Kirchner.

nung, die absolute Dummheit der Stoffwahl, lauter Dinge, die nach und nach den Charakter einer frechen Herausforderung jedes normalen, kunstinteressierten Beschauers annahmen.

Gruppe 2.

In diesen Räumen sind solche Bildwerke zusammengefaßt, die sich mit religiösen Inhalten befassen. Man nannte diese Schauerstücke in der jüdischen Presse einstmals „Offenbarungen deutscher Religiosität". Der normal empfindende Mensch denkt allerdings bei diesen „Offenbarungen" eher an einen Hexenspuk und empfindet sie, ganz gleich, welchem religiösen Bekenntnis er angehört, als unverschämten Hohn auf jede religiöse Vorstellung. Außerordentlich beachtenswert ist die Tatsache, daß gemalte und geschnitzte Verhöhnungen jüdisch-alttestamentarischer Legenden nicht anzutreffen sind. Die

---

Bis zum Machtantritt des Nationalsozialismus hat es in Deutschland eine sogenannte „moderne" Kunst gegeben, d. h. also, wie es schon im Wesen dieses Wortes liegt, fast jedes Jahr eine andere. Das nationalsozialistische Deutschland aber will wieder eine deutsche Kunst, und diese soll und wird wie alle schöpferischen Werte eines Volkes eine ewige sein. Entbehrt sie aber eines solchen Ewigkeitswertes für unser Volk, dann ist sie auch heute ohne höheren Wert.

Der Führer
bei der Eröffnung des Hauses der Deutschen Kunst.

„Offenbarungen deutscher Religiosität"

hat die den jüdischen Kunsthändlern feile Presse einmal solchen Hexenspuk genannt.

Die Titel lauten:

„Christus und die Sünderin", „Tod der Maria aus Ägypten". „Kreuzabnahme" und „Christus".
Die „Künstler" heißen: Nolde, Morgner und Kurth.

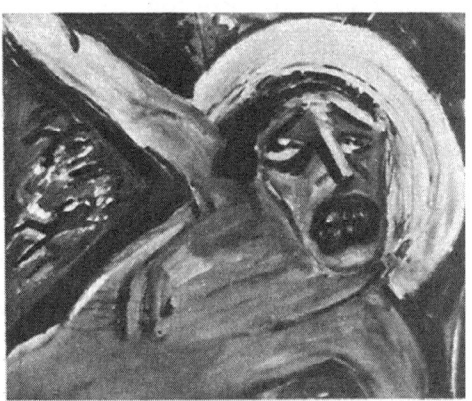

Gestalten der christlichen Legende hingegen grinsen uns hier mit immer neuen Teufelsfratzen an.

Gruppe 3.

Die in dieser Abteilung gezeigten Graphiken sind schlüssige Beweise für den politischen Hintergrund der Kunstentartung. Mit den Ausdrucksmitteln einer künstlerischen Anarchie wird hier die politische Anarchie als Forderung gepredigt. Jedes einzelne Bild dieser Gruppe ruft zum Klassenkampf im Sinne des Bolschewismus auf. Der schaffende Mensch soll durch eine grob tendenziöse Proletkunst gestärkt werden in der Überzeugung, daß er so lange ein in geistigen Ketten schmachtender Sklave bleiben wird, bis auch der letzte Besitzende, der letzte Nichtproletarier von der erhofften bolschewistischen Revolution beseitigt sein wird. Mit grauen und grünen Elendsgesichtern starren Arbeiter, Arbeiterfrauen und Arbeiterkinder dem Beschauer entgegen. Auf

---

> Die nationalsozialistische Bewegung und Staatsführung darf auch auf kulturellem Gebiet nicht dulden, daß Nichtskönner oder Gaukler plötzlich ihre Fahne wechseln und so, als ob nichts gewesen wäre, in den neuen Staat einziehen, um dort auf dem Gebiete der Kunst und Kulturpolitik abermals das große Wort zu führen.
>
> Der Führer
> Reichsparteitag 1933

Degenerate Art

den Zeichnungen sind alle überhaupt nur vorstellbaren „Kapitalisten" und „Ausbeuter" dargestellt, wie sie sich höhnend über das Elend des schaffenden Menschen hinwegsetzen. Vom Fleischermeister bis zum Bankier sind alle diese „Sklavenhalter" dargestellt. Nur jene sicherlich damals auch nicht darbenden jüdischen Kunsthändler, die sich gerade auch an dieser Proletkunst nicht wenig bereicherten, sind auffälligerweise von den Klassenkampfmalern ganz übersehen worden.

Gruppe 4.

Auch diese Abteilung hat eine ausgeprägte p o l i t i s c h e T e n d e n z. Hier tritt die „Kunst" in den Dienst der marxistischen Propaganda für die Wehrpflichtverweigerung. Die Absicht tritt klar zutage: Der Beschauer soll im Soldaten den Mörder oder das sinnlose Schlachtopfer einer im Sinn des bolschewistischen Klassen= kampfes „kapitalistischen Weltordnung" erblicken. Vor allem aber soll dem Volk die tief eingewurzelte Achtung vor jeder soldatischen Tugend, vor Mut, Tapferkeit und Einsatzbereitschaft ausgetrieben werden. So sehen wir in den Zeichnungen dieser Abteilung neben bewußt Abscheu erregenden Zerrbildern von Kriegskrüppeln und den mit aller Raffinesse ausgemalten Einblicken in Massengräber die

---

Eine Kunst, die nicht auf die freudigste und innigste Zustimmung der gesunden breiten Masse des Volkes rechnen kann, sondern sich nur auf kleine, teils interessierte, teils blasierte Cliquen stützt, ist unerträglich. Sie versucht das gesunde, instinktsichere Gefühl eines Volkes zu verwirren, statt es freudig zu unterstützen.

Der Führer
bei der Eröffnung des Hauses der Deutschen Kunst.

Degenerate Art

„Der Künstler muß als Künstler Anarchist sein."
Der Jude und Bolschewist Kurt Eisner, München, in „Aufruf zum Sozialismus".

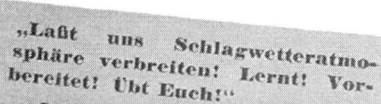

„Laßt uns Schlagwetteratmosphäre verbreiten! Lernt! Vorbereitet! Übt Euch!"
Der Bolschewist Johann R. Becher in „Aufruf an alle Künstler" 1919, Berlin.

deutschen Soldaten als Trottel, gemeine erotische Wüstlinge und Säufer dargestellt. Daß nicht nur Juden, sondern auch deutschblütige „Künstler" mit solch niederträchtigen Machwerken die feindliche Kriegsgreuelpropaganda, die damals schon als Lügengewebe entlarvt war, nachträglich auf diese Weise unaufgefordert erneut bestätigten, wird für immer ein Schandfleck der deutschen Kulturgeschichte bleiben.

Gruppe 5.

Diese Abteilung der Ausstellung gibt einen Einblick in die moralische Seite der Kunstentartung. Für die darin vertretenen „Künstler" ist offensichtlich die ganze Welt ein einziges großes Bordell, und die Menschheit setzt sich für sie aus lauter Dirnen und Zuhältern zusammen. Es gibt unter dieser gemalten und gezeichneten Pornographie Blätter und Bilder, die man auch im Rahmen der Ausstellung „Entartete Kunst" nicht mehr zeigen kann, wenn man daran denkt, daß auch Frauen diese Schau besuchen werden. Es ist für jeden Menschen unseres heutigen Deutschlands völlig unbegreiflich, daß man vor wenigen Jahren noch, und zwar auch noch in den Zeiten der Zentrumsherrschaft unter Heinrich Brüning, so abgrundtiefe Gemeinheiten, so viel Verkommenheit und ein so eindeutig überführtes Verbrechertum unter der Devise „Freiheit der Kunst" ungehindert an die niedersten Instinkte des Untermenschentums appellieren ließ. Das aber darf nicht übersehen werden: Auch diese Seite der Kunstentartung geht letzten Endes auf eine politische Zielstellung zurück. Das ist schon daraus ersichtlich, daß fast alle diese Schweinereien auch eine deutliche marxistisch-klassenkämpferische Tendenz aufweisen. Immer wieder begegnet man Blättern, auf denen Wüstlinge der „besitzenden Klasse" und ihre Dirnen in Gegensatz gestellt sind zu den ausgehungerten Gestalten des im Hintergrunde sich müde vorbeischleppenden „Proletariats". Auf anderen Zeichnungen wird die Dirne idealisiert und in Gegensatz gestellt zur Frau der bürgerlichen Gesellschaft, die nach Ansicht der Macher dieser „Kunst" moralisch viel

Gemalte Wehrsabotage
des Malers Otto Dix

verworfener ist als die Prostituierte. Kurzum: **Das moralische Programm des Bolschewismus schreit in dieser Abteilung von allen Wänden.**

Gruppe 6.

Hier wird an einer größeren Zahl von Werken sichtbar gemacht, daß sich die entartete Kunst vielfach auch in den Dienst jenes Teiles der marxistischen und bolschewistischen Ideologie gestellt hat, deren Ziel lautet: Planmäßige **Abtötung der letzten Reste jedes Rassebewußtseins**. Wurde in den Bildern der vorigen Abteilung die Dirne als sittliches Ideal hingestellt, so begegnen wir nun hier dem **Neger und Südseeinsulaner** als dem offensichtlichen **rassischen Ideal** der „modernen Kunst". Es ist kaum zu glauben, daß die Macher

---

Und was fabrizieren sie? Mißgestaltete Krüppel und Kretins, Frauen, die nur abscheuerregend wirken können, Männer, die Tieren näher sind als Menschen, Kinder, die, wenn sie so leben würden, geradezu als Fluch Gottes empfunden werden müßten! Und das wagen diese grausamsten Dilettanten unserer heutigen Mitwelt als die Kunst unserer Zeit vorzustellen, d. h. als den Ausdruck dessen, was die heutige Zeit gestaltet und ihr den Stempel aufprägt.

Der Führer
bei der Eröffnung des Hauses der Deutschen Kunst
über die Träger des Kunstzerfalles.

Die Dirne wird zum sittlichen Ideal erhoben!

Was die bolschewistische Jüdin Rosa Luxemburg an der russischen Literatur besonders liebte: „Die russische Literatur adelt die Prostituierte, verschafft ihr Genugtuung für das an ihr begangene Verbrechen der Gesellschaft…, erhebt sie aus dem Fegefeuer der Korruption und ihrer seelischen Qualen in die Höhe sittlicher Reinheit und weiblichen Heldentums."

Rosa Luxemburg in „Die Aktion" 1921.

dieser Bildwerke in Deutschland oder in Europa ihre Heimat haben oder wenigstens damals noch hatten. Dabei ist allerdings zu betonen, daß auch diese Niggerkunst handwerklich so barbarisch ist, daß sich mancher Neger mit Recht dagegen auflehnen würde, in den dargestellten Gestalten Menschen seinesgleichen zu erblicken oder gar der Urheberschaft an solchen Bildwerken bezichtigt zu werden.

Gruppe 7.

In dieser Abteilung der Ausstellung wird klar gemacht, daß außer dem Neger als dem rassischen Ideal der damals „modernen" Kunst auch ein ganz besonders **geistiges Ideal** vorschwebte, nämlich der **Idiot**, der **Kretin** und der **Paralytiker**. Auch wo sich diese „Künstler" selbst oder gegenseitig porträtierten, kommen dabei ausgesprochen kretinhafte Gesichter und Gestalten heraus. Das mag, den übrigen Werken nach zu schließen, nicht immer ein grundsätzlicher Verzicht auf Ähnlichkeit sein. Sicher aber ist, daß jedes stupid-idiotenhafte Gesicht die hier vertretenen „Modernen" **besonders** zum Schaffen angeregt hat. Anders wäre es nicht zu erklären, daß auch diese Abteilung der Ausstellung in Plastik, Graphik und Malerei so umfangreich ist. Hier sind

---

„Kunstwerke", die an sich nicht verstanden werden können, sondern als Daseinsberechtigung erst eine schwulstige Gebrauchsanweisung benötigen, um endlich jenen Verschüchterten zu finden, der einen so dummen oder frechen Unsinn geduldig aufnimmt, werden von jetzt ab den Weg zum deutschen Volke nicht mehr finden.

Der Führer
bei der Eröffnung des Hauses der Deutschen Kunst
über die entartete Kunst.

Degenerate Art

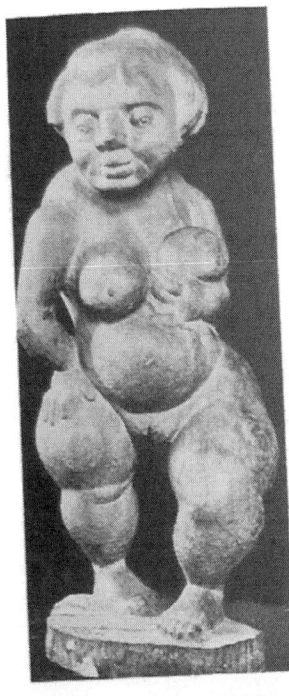

Jeder Kommentar ist hier überflüssig!

Die „Werke" stammen von Voll, Kirchner, Heckel, Hoffmann und Schmidt-Rottluff.

menschliche Figuren zu sehen, die wahrhaftig mit Gorillas mehr Ähnlichkeit haben als mit Menschen. Hier gibt es Porträts, gegen die die ersten geschichtlich bekannten Versuche der Menschendarstellung in steinzeitlichen Höhlen reife Meisterwerke sind. A b e r a u c h   f ü r   s o l c h e   S c h a u e r s t ü c k e   w u r d e n ,   w i e d i e A n k a u f s p r e i s e   a u s w e i s e n ,   n o c h   v o r   w e n i g e n J a h r e n   h ö c h s t e   P r e i s e   v e r l a n g t   u n d   b e z a h l t .

Gruppe 8.

In einem kleinen Raum sind hier der Abwechslung halber einmal n u r J u d e n vertreten. Damit keine Mißverständnisse entstehen, sei bemerkt, daß es sich hier nur um eine kleine Auswahl aus den zahlreichen jüdischen Machwerken handelt, die die Ausstellung insgesamt zeigt. Die großen „Verdienste", die sich die jüdischen Wortführer, Händler und Förderer der entarteten Kunst zweifellos erworben haben, rechtfertigt zur Genüge diese „S o n d e r e h r u n g". Hier findet sich u. a. auch „Der neue Mensch", wie ihn sich Jud F r e u n d l i c h erträumt hat. Dort

---

Das Judentum verstand es, besonders unter Ausnützung seiner Stellung in der Presse, mit Hilfe der sogenannten Kunstkritik nicht nur die natürlichen Auffassungen über das Wesen und die Aufgaben der Kunst sowie deren Zweck allmählich zu verwirren, sondern überhaupt das allgemeine gesunde Empfinden auf diesem Gebiete zu zerstören.

Der Führer
bei der Eröffnung des Hauses der Deutschen Kunst.

Drei Kostproben von jüdischer Plastik und Malerei

Die Titel lauten:
„Selbstbildnis", „Der neue Mensch" und „Kopf".

Die Juden heißen:
Meidner, Freundlich und Haizmann.

stehen und hängen auch noch andere plastische und gemalte Wüstenträume herum, denen gegenüber Worte versagen müssen.

Gruppe 9.

Dieser Abteilung kann man nur die Überschrift „Vollendeter Wahnsinn" geben. Sie nimmt den größten Raum der Ausstellung ein und enthält einen Querschnitt durch die Ausgeburten sämtlicher „Ismen", die Flechtheim, Wollheim und Cohnsorten im Laufe der Jahre ausgeheckt, gefördert und verramscht haben. Auf den Bildern und Zeichnungen dieses Schauerkabinetts ist meistens überhaupt nicht mehr zu erkennen, was den kranken Geistern vorschwebte, als sie zu Pinsel oder Stift gegriffen. Der eine „malte" schließlich nur noch mit dem Inhalt von Mülleimern. Ein anderer begnügte sich mit drei schwarzen Linien und einem Stück Holz auf einem großen weißen Untergrund. Ein Dritter hatte die Erleuchtung, „Einige Kreise" auf zwei Quadratmeter Leinwand zu malen. Ein Vierter verbrauchte nacheinander für drei Selbstbildnisse gut drei Kilogramm Farbe, da er sich nicht einig werden konnte, ob sein Kopf grün oder schwefelgelb, rund oder eckig, seine Augen rot oder himmelblau oder sonst etwas sind. In dieser Gruppe des Wahnsinns pflegen die Ausstellungsbesucher nur noch den Kopf zu schütteln und zu lachen. Sicher nicht ohne Grund. Aber wenn man bedenkt, daß auch all diese „Kunstwerke" nicht etwa aus verstaubten Ecken verlassener Ateliers, sondern aus den Kunstsammlungen und Museen der großen deutschen Städte herausgeholt wurden, wo sie teilweise noch in den ersten Jahren nach der Machtergreifung hingen und der staunenden Mitwelt dargeboten wurden, dann kann man nicht mehr lachen: dann kann man nur mit der Wut darüber kämpfen, daß mit einem so anständigen Volk wie dem deutschen überhaupt einmal so Schindluder getrieben werden konnte.

Selbst das wurde einmal ernst genommen und hoch bezahlt!

Die Titel heißen: „Der Gott der Flieger", „Am Strand", „Merzbild" und „Familienbild".

Die „Künstler" heißen: Molzahn, Metzinger und Schwitters.

Kunstbolschewismus am Ende.

Aus der Rede des Führers zur Eröffnung des Hauses der Deutschen Kunst in München.

Ich will in dieser Stunde bekennen, daß es mein unabänderlicher Entschluß ist, genau so wie auf dem Gebiet der politischen Verwirrung nunmehr auch hier mit den Phrasen im deutschen Kunstleben aufzuräumen.

„Kunstwerke", die an sich nicht verstanden werden können, sondern als Daseinsberechtigung erst eine schwulstige Gebrauchsanweisung benötigen, um endlich jenen Verschüchterten zu finden, der einen so dummen oder frechen Unsinn geduldig aufnimmt, werden von jetzt ab den Weg zum deutschen Volke nicht mehr finden!

Alle diese Schlagworte, wie: „inneres Erleben", „eine starke Gesinnung", „kraftvolles Wollen", „zukunftsträchtige Empfindung", „heroische Haltung", „bedeutsames Einfühlen", „erlebte Zeitordnung", „ursprüngliche Primitivität" usw., alle diese dummen, verlogenen Ausreden, Phrasen oder Schwätzereien, werden keine Entschuldigung oder gar Empfehlung für an sich wertlose, weil einfach ungekonnte Erzeugnisse mehr abgeben.

Ob jemand ein starkes Wollen hat oder ein inneres Erleben, das mag er durch sein Werk und nicht durch schwatzhafte Worte beweisen. Überhaupt interessiert uns alle viel weniger das sogenannte Wollen als das Können. Es muß daher ein Künstler, der damit rechnet, in diesem Haus zur Ausstellung zu kommen oder überhaupt noch in Zukunft in Deutschland aufzutreten, über ein Können verfügen. Das Wollen ist doch wohl von vornherein selbstverständlich! Denn es wäre schon das Allerhöchste, wenn ein Mensch seine Mitbürger mit Arbeiten belästigte, in denen er am Ende nicht einmal was wollte. Wenn diese Schwätzer nun aber ihre Werke dadurch schmackhaft zu machen versuchen, daß sie sie eben als den Ausdruck einer neuen Zeit hinstellen, so kann ihnen nur gesagt werden, daß nicht die Kunst neue Zeiten schafft, sondern daß sich das allgemeine Leben der Völker neu gestaltet und daher oft auch nach einem neuen

Degenerate Art

Zwei „Heilige"!!
Die obere heißt „Die Heilige vom inneren Licht" und stammt von Paul Klee. Die untere stammt von einem Schizophrenen aus einer Irrenanstalt. Daß diese „Heilige Magdalena mit Kind" immer noch menschenähnlicher aussieht als das Machwerk von Paul Klee, das durchaus ernst genommen werden wollte, ist sehr aufschlußreich.

„**Ethik der Geisteskrankheit.**"
„Der Besessenen wahnsinniges Reden ist die höhere Weltweisheit, da sie menschlich ist ... Warum haben wir diese Einsicht gegenüber der Welt des freien Willens noch nicht gewonnen? Weil wir äußerlich die Herren des Wahnsinns sind, weil die Geisteskranken von uns vergewaltigt werden, und wir sie daran hindern, nach ihren ethischen Gesetzen zu leben ... Jetzt müssen wir den toten Punkt in unserem Verhältnis zur Geisteskrankheit zu überwinden trachten."
Der Jude Wieland Herzfelde in „Die Aktion" 1914.

Ausdruck sucht. Allein, das, was in den letzten Jahrzehnten in Deutschland von einer neuen Kunst redete, hat die neue deutsche Zeit jedenfalls nicht begriffen. Denn nicht Literaten sind die Gestalter einer neuen Epoche, sondern die Kämpfer, d. h. die wirklich gestaltenden völkerführenden und damit Geschichte machenden Erscheinungen. Dazu werden sich aber diese armseligen verworrenen Pinsler oder Skribenten wohl kaum rechnen.

Außerdem ist es entweder eine unverfrorene Frechheit oder eine schwer begreifliche Dummheit, ausgerechnet unserer heutigen Zeit Werke vorzusetzen, die vielleicht vor zehn- oder zwanzigtausend Jahren von einem Steinzeitler hätten gemacht werden können. Sie reden von einer Primitivität der Kunst, und sie vergessen dabei ganz, daß es nicht die Aufgabe der Kunst ist, sich von der Entwicklung eines Volkes nach rückwärts zu entfernen, sondern daß es nur ihre Aufgabe sein kann, diese lebendige Entwicklung zu symbolisieren.

Die heutige neue Zeit arbeitet an einem neuen Menschentyp. Ungeheure Anstrengungen werden auf unzähligen Gebieten des Lebens vollbracht, um das Volk zu heben, um unsere Männer, Knaben und Jünglinge, die Mädchen und Frauen gesünder und damit kraftvoller und schöner zu gestalten. Und aus dieser Kraft und aus dieser Schönheit strömen ein neues Lebensgefühl, eine neue Lebensfreude. Niemals war die Menschheit im Aussehen und in ihrer Empfindung der Antike näher als heute. Sport-, Wett- und Kampfspiele stählen Millionen jugendlicher Körper und zeigen sie uns nun steigend in einer Form und Verfassung, wie sie vielleicht tausend Jahre lang nicht gesehen, ja kaum geahnt worden sind. Ein leuchtend schöner Menschentyp wächst heran, der nach höchster Arbeitsleistung dem schönen alten Spruch huldigt: Saure Wochen, aber frohe Feste. Dieser Menschentyp, den wir erst im vergangenen Jahr in den Olympischen Spielen in seiner strahlenden stolzen körperlichen Kraft und Gesundheit vor der ganzen Welt in Erscheinung treten sahen, dieser Menschentyp, meine Herren prähistorischen Kunststotterer, ist der Typ der neuen Zeit. Und was fabrizieren Sie? Mißgestaltete Krüppel und Kretins, Frauen, die nur abschenerregend wirken können, Männer, die Tieren näher sind als Menschen, Kinder, die, wenn

Degenerate Art

Dieser Mädchenkopf ist die Arbeit eines unheilbar irrsinnigen Mannes in der psychiatrischen Klinik in Heidelberg. Daß irrsinnige Nichtkünstler solche Bildwerke schaffen, ist verständlich.

Diese Spottgeburt aber wurde ehedem ernsthaft als Kunstwerk besprochen und stand als Meisterwerk von E. Hoffmann in vielen Kunstausstellungen der Vergangenheit. Der Titel des Monstrums hieß: „Mädchen mit blauem Haar"; seine Frisur erstrahlt nämlich in reinstem Himmelblau.

sie so leben würden, geradezu als Fluch Gottes empfunden werden
müßten! Und das wagen diese grausamsten Dilletanten unserer heutigen Mitwelt als die Kunst unserer Zeit vorzustellen, d. h. als den
Ausdruck dessen, was die heutige Zeit gestaltet und ihr den Stempel
aufprägt.

Man sage nur nicht, daß diese Künstler das eben so sehen.
Ich habe hier unter den eingeschickten Bildern manche Arbeiten be-
obachtet, bei denen tatsächlich angenommen werden muß, das ge-
wissen Menschen das Auge die Dinge anders zeigt, als sie sind, d. h.,
daß es wirklich Männer gibt, die die heutigen Gestalten unseres
Volkes nur als verkommene Kretins sehen, die grundsächlich Wiesen
blau, Himmel grün, Wolken schwefelgelb usw. empfinden oder, wie
sie vielleicht sagen, erleben. Ich will mich nicht in einen Streit darüber einlassen, ob diese Betreffenden das nun wirklich so sehen und
empfinden oder nicht, sondern ich möchte im Namen des deutschen
Volkes es nur verbieten, das so bedauerliche Unglückliche, die ersichtlich an Sehstörungen leiden, die Ergebnisse ihrer Fehlbetrachtung

---

Fest stand der Entschluß, die dadaistisch-kubi-
stischen und futuristischen Erlebnis- und
Sachlichkeitsschwätzer unter keinen Umständen
an unserer kulturellen Neugeburt teilnehmen
zu lassen. Dies wird die wirkungsvollste Folge-
rung aus der Erkenntnis der Art des hinter uns
liegenden Kulturzerfalls sein.

Der Führer
Reichsparteitag 1935

Degenerate Art

Wenn ein unheilbar Irrsinniger,
ein Dilettant wohlgemerkt, eine Katze modelliert, so sieht das etwa so aus:

Wenn dagegen der Jude Haizmann,
der seinerzeit als ein „genialer Plastiker" gefeiert wurde, auf die Idee kommt, ein „Fabeltier" zu schaffen, so sieht dieses als Brunnenfigur gedachte Monstrum so aus, wie dieses Bild zeigt:

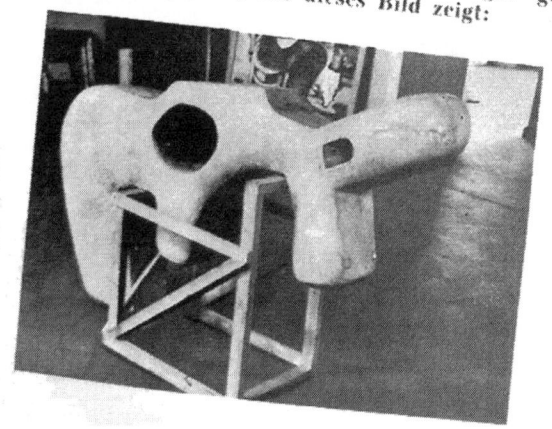

Das Judengeschöpf wiegt nebenbei bemerkt etliche Zentner.

der Mitwelt mit Gewalt als Wirklichkeiten aufzuschwätzen versuchen, oder ihr gar als „Kunst" vorsetzen wollen.

Nein, hier gibt es nur zwei Möglichkeiten: Entweder diese sogenannten „Künstler" sehen die Dinge wirklich so und glauben daher an das, was sie darstellen, dann wäre nur zu untersuchen, ob ihre Augenfehler entweder auf mechanische Weise oder durch Vererbung zustande gekommen sind. Im einen Fall tief bedauerlich für diese Unglücklichen, im zweiten wichtig für das Reichsinnenministerium, das sich dann mit der Frage zu beschäftigen hätte, wenigstens eine weitere Vererbung derartiger grauenhafter Sehstörungen zu unterbinden. Oder aber sie glauben selbst nicht an die Wirklichkeit solcher Eindrücke, sondern sie bemühen sich aus anderen Gründen, die Nation mit diesem Humbug zu belästigen, dann fällt so ein Vorgehen in das Gebiet der Strafrechtspflege.... Es interessiert mich dabei auch nicht im geringsten, ob sich diese Auch-Künstler die von ihnen gelegten Eier dann gegenseitig begackern und damit begutachten oder nicht! Denn der Künstler schafft nicht für den Künstler, sondern er schafft genau so wie alle Anderen für das Volk! Und wir werden dafür Sorge tragen, daß gerade das Volk von jetzt ab wieder zum Richter über seine Kunst aufgerufen wird.

Durch bewußte Verrücktheiten sich auszuzeichnen, um damit die Aufmerksamkeit zu erringen, das zeugt nicht nur von einem künstlerischen Versagen, sondern auch von einem moralischen Defekt.

Der Führer
Reichsparteitag 1933

Degenerate Art

Welche von diesen drei
Zeichnungen ist wohl eine Dilettantenarbeit vom Insassen eines Irrenhauses?

Staunen Sie: Die r e c h t e o b e r e ! Die beiden anderen dagegen wurden einst als meisterliche Graphiken K o k o s c h k a s bezeichnet.

Entartete Kunst

Dummheit oder Frechheit — oder beides — auf die Spitze getrieben!

Ein wertvolles Geständnis:
„Wir können bluffen wie die abgesottensten Pokerspieler. Wir tun so, als ob wir Maler, Dichter oder sonst was wären, aber wir sind nur und nichts als mit Wollust frech. Wir setzen aus Frechheit einen riesigen Schwindel in die Welt und züchten Snobs, die uns die Stiefel abschlecken, parce que c'est notre plaisir. Windmacher, Sturmmacher sind wir mit unserer Frechheit."

Aus dem Manifest von A. Undo in „Die Aktion" 1915.

ENGLISH TRANSLATION

Entartete Kunst

Above: The Dada display, and below, an advertising poster.

Guide

to the Exhibition

Degenerate Art

The exhibition was compiled by the Reich Propaganda Office, Cultural section. It will be shown in the larger cities of all provinces. Responsibility for contents: Fritz Kaiser, Munich. Publisher: Publishing House for Culture and Commercial Advertising, 59 Potsdamer Street, Berlin W 35, 59.

Entartete Kunst

What is the aim of "Degenerate Art" exhibition?

It aims to start a new era for the German people, by providing through the display of original works, an insight into the harrowing cultural decay which took place during the decades which preceded the Great Change.

It aims to put an end to the endless chattering by some writers and cliques who, still today, deny that there was any degeneration in art forms.

It aims to make it clear that this degeneration of art was more than that just a passing rush of a few fools, follies, and experiments, which only died out with the coming of the National Socialist Revolution.

It aims to show that this was not a "natural progression" of culture, but a planned attack on the essence and continued existence of art in general.

It aims to show the common root of political anarchy and cultural anarchy, which exposes degenerate art as Bolshevist in every sense of the word.

It aims to show the ideological, political, racial intentions and moral goals which were the driving forces behind the degeneration.

It will also demonstrate the extent to which this deliberately driven degeneracy attracted imitators, who, despite the latter's earlier and sometimes later proven certain talent, character, joined in with this overall Jewish and Bolshevist nonsense.

It will show how some of the more dangerous Jewish and political leaders were able to attract a person, who might have rejected party political Bolshevism out of hand, into the service of that ideology through cultural anarchy.

Degenerate Art

"Art which can be called a communist, passed through two phases:
1. It takes place in the Communist Party, and the obligations of solidarity in the struggle;
2. It carries out the revolutionary rearrangement of production."
The Jew Wieland Herzfelde in "The Opponent" 1920/21.

It aims to conclusively prove that this consciously degenerate art was produced by adults and was not the "harmless folly of youth."

Furthermore, the "Degenerate Art" exhibition does:

Not want to claim that all the names of artists attached to works in the exhibition are members of the Communist Party. It is not necessary for a refutation to be made, as no such claim is intended.

Not want to deny that one or the other of the persons represented here sometimes - sooner or later – also could have worked "skillfully or differently."
Nor can the exhibition conceal the fact that these men were in the forefront of the general Bolshevik degenerate attack on German art.

Not want to prevent those of German blood whose work is included in the exhibition, who have not followed their Jewish friends of old into foreign lands, from now engaging in an honest struggle and helping the fight for a new and healthy art movement.

It does and must mean to prevent, however, the jabbering cliques from that murky part from foisting any such men on the new state and on its forward-looking people as "the natural standard-bearers of an art of the Third Reich."

Degenerate Art

"We prefer to exist squalidly, rather than to perish in cleanliness. Incapable of being decent, we leave individualism to the stubborn and the old maids. Nothing to fear about good reputations."—"The Opponent" 1920/21.

"Realism is divided and broken up as a receptacle for his pent-up, sensual burning passion. The—now exhausted—parts are joined together with a lack of emotional depth, and in their outward form, are all-consuming and expansive. No more resistance is offered and there are no more high borders to overcome..." - Contemporary literary commentary on "modern" brothel art.

The Structure of the Exhibition

The abundance of degenerate are makes a devastating impression upon all visitors. This is created by grouping all the related works in individual rooms. Below, the outline is briefly presented:

Group 1

This is a general overview to illustrate the barbarity of the representation of small-scale point of view. One sees in this group the progressive decomposition of shape and color perception, the conscious contempt of basic skill in fine art, the flashy daubing of color in addition to the deliberate distortion of the drawing and the absolute stupidity of the subject.

Anyone who seeks the new for its own sake will easily be lost in folly's realm. Today, the most stupid art work, made from stone and other materials, might easily be considered as new. But in previous centuries, fools were not allowed to insult society with their sick-minded creations.

The Führer
Reich Party Congress 1933.

Degenerate Art

A very revealing racial cross-section

Note in particular the three painters' portraits shown below. They are, from left to right: the painter Morgner, as seen by himself the painter Radziwill, as seen by Otto Dix; and the painter Schlemmer as seen by E.L. Kirchner.

Entartete Kunst

All these things are characteristic of a bold challenge to any normal observer with an interest in art.

Group 2

In this section, works have been grouped together which deal with religious content involved. The Jewish press used to call these dreadful objects "German religious revelations." The normal religious person, no matter to which denomination they might adhere, can only consider these "revelations" as nothing but a nightmare and an outrageous mockery of the religious concept.

> Before the National Socialists came to power in Germany there was something called "modern" art, or as the word "modern" implies, almost every year there was a different kind of art. National Socialist Germany, however, wants "German art" again and this, like all creative values of a People, should be and will be art which is eternal. If it lacks this everlasting value for our People then today it also lacks any higher value.
>
> The Führer
> At the Opening of the
> House of German Art, 1937

Degenerate Art

Examples of "German Religiousness"
Is how the Jewish art dealers and their press described this witches' brew.

They are titled: "Christ and Adulteress," "Death of Mary of Egypt," "Deposition," and "Christ." The "artists" are: Nolde, Morgner, and Kurth.

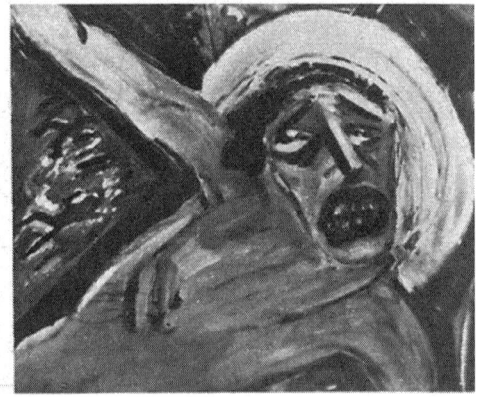

It is extremely noteworthy that painted and carved insults to the Jewish Old Testament legends are not to be found. The figures of Christian legends, however, leer at us with all manner of devil's faces.

Group 3

The graphics shown in this group are conclusive evidence of the political background to degenerate art. Political anarchy is preached as a form of artistic anarchy. Every picture in this group is a call for class struggle within the meaning of Bolshevism.

The creative person is subjected to a grossly tendentious Proletarian art form through which it is claimed that all will remain in mental and physical slavery until the last private property and the last non-Proletarian is eliminated.

The gray and green faces of miserable working men, women and children, stare out at the beholder.

> The National Socialist movement and government must not allow incompetents and charlatans in the field of culture to suddenly change sides and enlist under the banner of the new state as if nothing has happened, so that they cannot again influence art and cultural policy.
> The Führer
> Reich Party Congress 1933

"Art" Preaches Class War

"Artist, you want to overturn the world; you are a politician! Or you remain a private person . . . Painting for painting's sake is like having a rowing machine in your room." The anarchist Ludwig Rubiner in "Painters Build Barricades" ("Action," 1914)

Entartete Kunst

In these drawings, all manner of "capitalists" and "exploiters," from the butcher to the banker are depicted as mocking and ignoring the plight of the common working people. The Jewish art dealers, who were not exactly starving and who were greatly enriched by this Proletarian art, are conspicuously overlook by the painters of this class struggle.

Group 4

This group also displays a strong political bias. Here the "art" has been utilized in the service of Marxist propaganda to refuse military service. The clear intention to portray to the viewer an impression that soldiers are either murderers or senseless sacrifices, all within the context of Bolshevist class war against the "capitalist world order." Most of all, however, the aim is to expunge all notions of deep-rooted respect for a soldier's virtue, courage and bravery. Thus the drawings we see in this section contain deliberately repulsive views of horror and mass graves, while German soldiers are portrayed as fools, drunkards and low erotic-driven brutes.

> Art that cannot count on the joyous and inner support of the healthy masses, but depends on tiny cliques, only partly interested and partly blasé, is intolerable. It seeks to confuse the healthy and instinctive peoples' sentiment, instead of joyously reassuring it.
> The Führer
> At the Opening of the
> House of German Art, 1937.

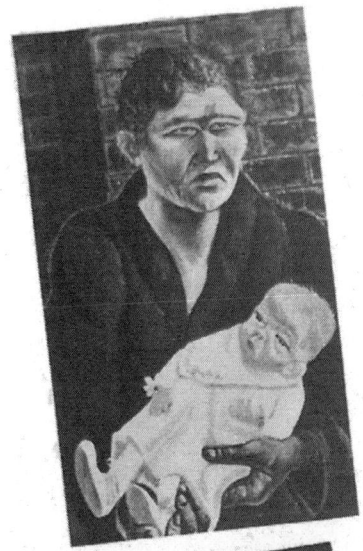

"The Artist must be an anarchist artist."
The Jew and Bolshevik Kurt Eisner, Munich, in "Appeal for Socialism."

"Let us create an incendiary atmosphere! Learn! Prepare! Practice!"
The Bolshevik John R. Becher in "Appeal to All Artists," 1919 Berlin.

Entartete Kunst

It will forever remain as a blot on the history of German culture that it was not only Jews but also German "artists" who engaged in such vile atrocity propaganda works which affirmed the enemy's propaganda, even though it had already been exposed as a web of lies.

Group 5

This section of the exhibition gives an insight into the moral side of degenerate art. The "artists" represent the whole world as one big brothel, and humanity as being made up of nothing but prostitutes and pimps.

Among these paintings and drawings are many pornographic images, which have been excluded from this show as because it will be seen by women as well.

It is for many people of present-day Germany quite incomprehensible that only a few years ago, during the times of the centrist regime of Heinrich Brüning, nothing was done to stop the abysmal depravity and obvious criminality which, under the guise of "Freedom of art," appealed to the Underman's lowest instincts.

But it should not be overlooked that degenerate art ultimately has a political dimension as its background. This is shown by the fact that almost all of this sloth shows significant tendencies in favour of a Marxist class war. Again and again, we encounter illustrations in which the brutish "owning class" and their whores are contrasted with the emaciated figures of the "Proletariat," who are portrayed as tired and sluggish.

In other drawings, the prostitute is idealized and contrasted with the woman of bourgeois society, who, in the opinion of the makers of this "art" are as morally depraved as the prostitutes.

Degenerate Art

Painted Military Sabotage
By the painter Otto Dix

In short, the moral Program of Bolshevism screams out loud from the walls in this section.

Group 6

The works shown in this section demonstrate that degenerate art is in service of that part of Marxist and Bolshevik ideology which seeks to destroy any last remnants of race consciousness.

In the previous section, the prostitute is portrayed as a moral ideal, and here we see how the Negro and the South Sea Islanders are presented at the racial ideal of "modern art." It is hard to believe that the makers of these sculptures had Germany or Europe as their home, or did so until recently.

> But what do you manufacture? Deformed cripples and cretins, women who inspire only disgust, men who are more like wild beasts, children who, if they were alive, would be regarded as God's curse! And this is what these cruel incompetents dare to present to us today as the art of our time, that is, as the expression of all that creates and sets its stamp on the present time.
> The Führer
> At the Opening of the
> House of German Art, 1937

The Prostitute Is Raised to an Ideal!

This is what the Bolshevik Jewess Rosa Luxembourg loved most about Russian literature: "Russian literature ennobles the prostitute, consoles her for the crime that society has committed against her, lifts her from the purgatory, corruption and torment of her soul to moral purity and female heroism."
Rosa Luxemburg in "Action" 1921.

Entartete Kunst

It is however important to emphasize that this nigger art is crafted in such a barbaric manner that even Negro would, justifiably, objected to see himself in these figures or even to be considered as the creator of such works.

Group 7

In this section of the exhibition it is made clear that, apart from the Negro, the next spiritual and racial idea envisaged by "modern" art is the idiot, the cretin and the cripple.

Also where these "artists" have depicted themselves or each other, they have always chosen to portray themselves with cretin-like faces and figures. That may be, if compared to other nearby sketches, not always reflect a denial of similarity.

But it is certain that every stupid-idiot-like face represented here, has served as the inspiration to "modern" work. Otherwise it would not be possible to explain why this section contains such an extensive collection of sculptures, paintings and graphics.

> "'Works of art' which cannot be understood, cannot speak for themselves but require a verbose set of instructions in order to find some shy creature who patiently listens to such stupid and brazen nonsense, will from now on no longer reach the German People."
> The Führer
> At the Opening of the
> House of German Art, 1937.

Comment is Superfluous here!

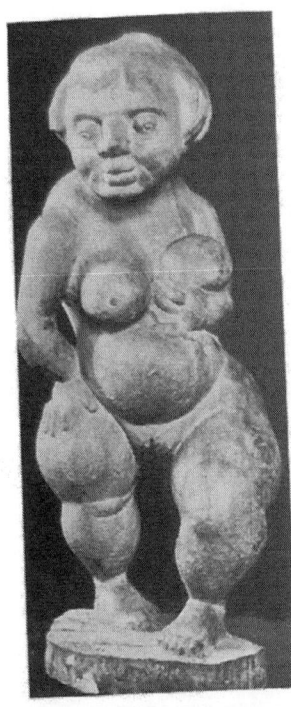

These "works" are by Voll, Kirchner, Heckel, Hoffmann, and Schmidt-Rottluff.

Entartete Kunst

These are human figures, which, if the truth is told, bear more in common with gorillas than with people. These portraits make the first known Stone Age attempts at representation of the human form seem like mature masterpieces. Incredibly, these pieces of nonsense commanded the highest prices just a few years ago, as indicated by their labels.

Group 8

In this small room, only Jewish artists are represented. To prevent any misunderstandings, it must be considered that this is only a small selection from the many Jewish concoctions which are in the exhibition. This "special honor" is justified because of the large "contribution" which Jewish spokesmen, traders and supporters made to the spread of degenerate art. In this section, for example, can be found "The new Man" as he was dreamed up by the Jew Freundlich.

> Jewry understood, especially through exploitation in the press, that with the help of so-called art critics, they could gradually obscure all natural perceptions of art's nature and responsibility, and also destroy its healthy sentiment.
> The Führer
> At the Opening of the
> House of German Art, 1937.

Three Samples of Degenerate Plasterwork and Painting

The titles are:
"Self-portrait" from the Jew Meidner,
"The New Man" sculpture from the Jew Freundlich,
"Head" by Haizmann.

There are also other plastic and painted pieces of waste on display, about which words must fail.

Group 9

This section can only be given the heading of "Accomplished Insanity." It forms the largest part of the exhibition and includes a cross-section of the spawn of all "isms" that Flechtheim, Wollheim and their colleagues have concocted, promoted and sold over the years. In the pictures and drawings on display in this room of nonsense, one cannot tell what was envisioned in their sick minds when they picked up their brushes or pencils.

One of them ended up painting only with the contents of garbage cans. Another was content with three black lines and a piece of wood on a large white surface. A third had the urge to paint "some circles" on two square meters of canvas. A fourth used over three kilograms of paint consecutively because he could not decide if his head should be green or sulfur-yellow, round or square, his eyes red or sky blue or something else.

In this part of the exhibition, visitors normally just shake their heads and laugh, and certainly not without reason. But when you consider that all this "art," was not in the dusty corners of abandoned studios, but were removed from display from the art collections and Museums of the large German cities (and some were still on display in the early years after the assumption of power by the Führer), then you can laugh no longer. Once can suppress one's anger at the fact that decent Germans could ever have been so exploited.

Degenerate Art

This was once taken seriously and commanded high prices!

The titles are: "The God of Airmen," "On the Bach," "Merz Picture," and "Family Portrait."
The "artists" are Molzahn, Metzinger and Schwitters.

Artistic Bolshevism at its End
From the Führer's speech at the opening of the House of German Art in Munich.

I would like to take this opportunity to state that I have made up my mind to put an end to meaningless phraseology in German art just as I did with confusion in politics. "Works of art" which cannot be understood, cannot speak for themselves but require a verbose set of instructions in order to find some shy creature who patiently listens to such stupid and brazen nonsense, will from now on no longer reach the German People.

All these catchy phrases such as "inner experience", "strong-minded", "a powerful desire", "feeling which is pregnant with the future", "heroic attitude", "significant intuitive powers", "inward experience of a system of time", "original primitivity" and so forth, all these stupid, fallacious excuses, phrases and meaningless formulations will not excuse or recommend products which are substandard and therefore without intrinsic value.

If someone has a strong will or inner experience, let him demonstrate this by his work, not by empty phrases. We are all far less interested in intentions than in ability. Therefore any artist who hopes to be exhibited in this building or has any desire to make a name for himself in Germany in the future, must have ability. The existence of a will to create something can be taken for granted! For that would really be the limit if someone were to foist upon his fellow citizens works which ultimately had no real purpose. If, however, these people with the gift of the gab try to make their works palatable by describing them as the expression of a new age, the only thing we can say to them is that it is not art which creates a new age. It is the general life of the People which takes on new forms and thus frequently seeks a new form of expression.

However, those who talked about new art in Germany in the last decades clearly did not understand the new age in Germany. For it is not the men who wield a pen who shape a new epoch, but those who are willing to enter the fray, who take control of the course of events, who lead their People and thus make history. These wretched, confused artists and scribes will hardly consider themselves men of this ilk.

Degenerate Art

Two "Saints"!

The one above is titled "The Saint of the Inner Light" and is by Paul Klee.

The one below is by a schizophrenic from a lunatic asylum. That is "Saint Mary Magdalena and Child' and it looks more human that the concoction by Paul Klee. That the latter is intended to be taken serious, is very telling.

"Ethics of Mental Illness"

"The crazy talk of the possessed is the higher wisdom, because it is human... Why have not yet gained this insight into the world of the free will? Because we are in command of insanity from the outside, because we violate the mentally ill and prevent them from living in accordance with their own ethical laws.... Now we must seek to overcome the blind spot in attitude towards mental illness."
The Hew Wieland Hezrzfelde, in "Action" 1914

People have attempted to recommend modern art by saying that it is the expression of a new age but art does not create a new age, it is the general life of peoples that fashions itself anew and often looks for a new expression... A new epoch is not created by littérateurs but by warriors, those who really fashion and lead the peoples and thus make history.

It is either impudent effrontery or an almost inconceivable stupidity to exhibit to people today works that might have been made by a man of the Stone Age perhaps ten or twenty thousand years ago. They talk of primitive art but they forget that it is not the function of art to retreat backwards from the development of a people: its sole function must be to symbolize that living development.

The new age of today is at work on a new human type. Incredible efforts are being made in many aspects of life, to exalt our people, our men, teenagers and boys. The girls and woman must be made healthier and therefore stronger and more beautiful. From this strength and beauty springs a new joy in life. Never has mankind been closer to antiquity, in appearance or in feeling, than it is today. Sport, competition and pretend is steeling millions of young bodies. They show us a form and condition that has not been seen and can scarcely have been imagined for a thousand years. A radiant and beautiful type of human being is growing, which after supreme achievement in work, honors that fine saying "Sour weeks but happy feats." This human type, as we saw him in last y ear's Olympic games, step out before the whole world in all the radiant pride of his bodily strength and health. This, my good prehistoric art stutterers, is the type of the new age, but what do you manufacture? Malformed cripples and cretins, women who inspire only disgust, men who are more like wild beasts, children who, were they alive, would have to be seen as cursed by God.

Degenerate Art

This girl's head is the work of an incurably insane inmate of the psychiatric clinic in Heidelberg. It is understandable that an insane non-artist should produce a work which looks like this.

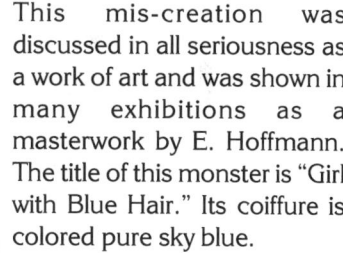

This mis-creation was discussed in all seriousness as a work of art and was shown in many exhibitions as a masterwork by E. Hoffmann. The title of this monster is "Girl with Blue Hair." Its coiffure is colored pure sky blue.

Entartete Kunst

This is what the cruel incompetents dare to present to us today as the art of our time, as the expression of all that creates and sets its stamp upon the present.

And let no one tell me that this is how these artists see things. From the pictures sent in for exhibition it is clear that the eye of some men portrays things otherwise than as they are, that there really are men who on principle feel meadows to be blue, the heavens green, clouds sulphur-yellow, or, as perhaps they prefer to say, 'experience' them thus.

I need not ask whether they really do see or feel things in this way, but in the name of the German people I have only to prevent these miserable unfortunates, who clearly suffer from defects of vision, from attempting violently to persuade contemporaries by their chatter that these faults of observation are indeed realities or from presenting them as 'art'.

> It is our firm decision that the Dadaist, Cubist and Futuristic experience and objectivity fools would never under any circumstances be allowed to take part in our cultural rebirth. This will be the most effective consequence from our understanding of the nature of the cultural decadence that lies behind us.
> The Führer
> Reich Party Congress 1935

Degenerate Art

When an incurable lunatic, and an amateur, please note, models a cat, this is how it looks:

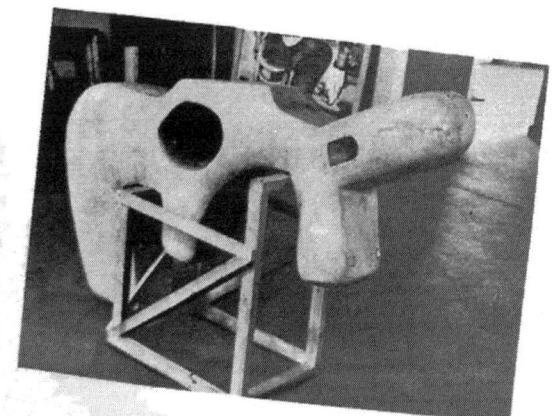

Bu Haizman on the contrary, praised in his own day as a "genius sculptor" had the idea to create a "fabulous animal" or a fountain head, created a monster which looked like this:

His concoction weighs several hundred kilograms, by the way.

There are only two possibilities here. Either these 'artists' really do see things in this way and believe in what they represent. Then one has only to ask how the defect in vision arose, and if it is hereditary the Minister for the Interior will have to see to it that so ghastly a defect of vision shall not be allowed to perpetuate itself. Or if they do not believe in the reality of such impressions but seek on other grounds to burden the nation with this humbug, then it is a matter for a criminal court . . . It does not interest me whether or not these so-called artists begin cackling over each other's eggs and given each other praise. The artist does not create for the artist. He creates for the people, and we shall see to it that the people in future will be called on to judge his art.

To draw attention to oneself by deliberate lunacies is not only a sight of artistic failure but also of moral defect.
The Führer
Reich Party Congress 1933.

Degenerate Art

Which of these three drawings is the work of an amateur artist who is also the inmate of a lunatic asylum?
Surprise! The one on the top right. The other two were regarded as masterly drawings by Kokoschka.

Extreme stupidity, imprudence or both

A valuable confession:
"We can bluff like the most hardened poker players. We can pretend to be painters, poets, or whatever, but if nothing else we are simply filled with impudent lust. Because of our impudence we perpetrate an enormous swindle upon the world, and we encourage snobs to lock our boots, because it is our pleasure. We are the impudent makers of storm and wind." From the manifesto by A. Undo in "Action" 1915.

Printed in Great Britain
by Amazon.co.uk, Ltd.,
Marston Gate.